ANCHOR
BOOKS

LOVE OF MY LIFE

Edited by

Rachael Radford

First published in Great Britain in 2003 by
ANCHOR BOOKS
Remus House,
Coltsfoot Drive,
Peterborough, PE2 9JX
Telephone (01733) 898102

HB ISBN 1 84418 094 8
SB ISBN 1 84418 095 6

FOREWORD

For many people poetry is a form of communication, used to express feelings to loved ones, family or friends.

This special anthology of creative poetry celebrates the gift of love in all its many guises, as each author shares their heartfelt feelings for another with you, the reader.

The subject of love varies greatly from poem to poem, be it for a partner, family member or friend.

This unique anthology is sure to entertain, this is a truly inspiring collection to be read time and time again.

Rachael Radford
Editor

CONTENTS

A Sunbeam For Jesus

Andrea, you had special charms
Laughing, crying, waving your arms
A sunbeam sent to your brother and me
We did not know how special you'd be
Soon learning to drink from a cup
Determined you were to sit up
Mum was bathing you one day
She pointed to a scar on your spine
It looked just like a thin line
You were bright and could talk
Mum said you might not ever walk

Then back from hospital came the news
An iron brace and special shoes
Could possible aid you to walk
You would try, there was a chance
To learn to walk or even dance
The last words you said to me
Were, 'Don't go out tonight She.'
Mum said, 'You must let Sheila go
She's played all day with you I know.'

When I got home there was a note
And a lump came to my throat
You had not been well at all
That night taking to Heaven your charms
You fell asleep in Mum's arms
Your headstone's a Bible inscribed the words
'A sunbeam for Jesus' this came true
When at eight and a half to Heaven you flew
Where a sunbeam lives life anew.

Sheila Walters

To My Dearest Dad

When I close my eyes at night,
I see the stars all shimmering bright,
And within each one I see the depth of your love,
And your face visualising through all the mist and cloud above.

When I'm depressed and my heartbeat is low,
I think of your smile and how every feature glows,
I envy the way you radiate love,
Your heart so warm and tender, just like a glove.

You are like the fire just flaring out,
Soaring through the richness of the earth, round about,
Nothing can stop the way you live,
But everything can glisten in the trail you give.

We are the rainbow and you are the gold,
That is one treasure that we can all hold.
So with kind wishes from all our hearts,
We love you and say thank you very, very much.

Bhavini Harish Haria (14)

THERE FOR ME

Don't think I don't know, the price you paid.
All of those sacrifices, that you made.

Being my rock, on which often I lent
Never will forget all of the hours, beside my sick bed spent.

The illness I had, caused in me such a deep hole
Had bitterness and anger deep within my soul

Although unable to express feelings to you,
I say on paper, thanks for staying and getting me through.

Now it's so sad, our feelings have inevitably been changed,
How could they, after all we went through, hope to stay the same.

A good friend to me you are now, always finding the time
To drop in, visit, check everything's just fine.

This poem is a way of showing, all of my appreciation,
Once again thanks with all my heart, for your care, your dedication.

Susan Barker

VERONICA

Vivacious and humorous,
Elegant in dress,
Relaxed and approachable,
Oblivious of stress.
Natural in gesture,
Instinctively correct,
Considerate at all times,
A friend to respect.

Some names have meanings, or so we are told,
Though the one I am murmuring has none to unfold.
Its owner for me is a source of delight
And my spirits revive when she ventures in sight.

R T Walker

I'D LIKE YOU TO KNOW

You are the lady in my life
You've been there for 50 years.
My only love, my only wife
So loyal and sincere.

We met when times were different
Than they are today
We had to earn before we spent
We struggled to pay our way.

We had two kids and brought them up
The only way we knew
With lots of caring love
And maybe just a smack or two.

The heart attack you suffered
Left me terrified
The joy when you recovered
Was so great I nearly cried.

50 years of loving you
Has kept me young at heart
I can't believe my luck that you too
Loved me from the start.

R S Hannam

The Best Gran Ever

My gran is caring, helpful and kind.
She has three pets, but I don't mind.
She likes to wind up Grandad,
Which makes him, very mad.

My gran is very pretty.
She is all so very witty.
She is talented and clever.
She is hurting when there is a change in the weather.

My gran is the best yet.
She will never change, I'll bet.

Emma Rose (11)

MY BEST FRIEND

I wish that you were here today
To put your arms around me
Holding me close
To give me comfort and support
Listening to my troubles
As only you know how
No one can take your place
You are very special
You were my best friend.

Alice Higham

My Son Stephen

Of you I am so very proud.
You will always stand out in a crowd.
Your sense of humour endears you to one and all.
So many happy memories I can recall.
I remember a little boy popular with the girls
who loved to twang your springy curls.
I marvelled at your mimicry.
You were fascinated by the adverts
and cartoons on TV.
I remember with your hands
you were creative.
Your mind was eternally
healthy and active.
Building models and drawing
complicated bomber attacks.
Your punishment for talking in class
was to draw freehand maps.
Your sense of fairplay can be admired.
To play the game you never tired.
You are a man packed full
of common-sense.
Even though at times you appear
crotchety and tense.
Children you have always adored.
With you they are never bored.
You act the part as if upon a stage.
Teasing and playing whatever their age.
Stephen you will never grow old
with your fun loving personality.

A gift from God.

Elizabeth Myra Crellin

Lisa

Our Lisa's looking slim;
She's been busy getting trim.
Losing weight looking great,
Taking off a stone in weight.
What it is to have willpower.
Counting points by the hour.
Checking plan to get it right.
No more snacks for her tonight!
She will get there in the end.
Neat and tidy my dear friend.

Lyn Peacock-Sayers

For You, Alison
On Your 40th Birthday

Thank you, for the joys, you've brought
Thank you for being you -
Thank you for each hour and thought,
For 40 years - good and true.

From baby days - to learning ways
To school and growing up fast,
Thinking back on ev'ry phase,
Memories of you, last . . .
First tooth, first steps
Delight at your first word, then
Music lessons, recorder playing -
Bottom of the garden, best place to be heard?
Brownies, guides, first-aid cadet,
Sunday school concerts - we just can't forget!
Kisses you gave me, when I went tired and slow
The welcome of those! Oh! The glow!
Cycle days, pedalling along with me, Dad and Sis
Youth hostelling in winter cold and summer bliss,
Gardening and planting - you were my right hand
Growing carrots, broad beans, sprouts, so tasty. Grand
You and I wallpapering - with care and delight,
Happiness and smiles, when we got it right,
That 'fat' brown envelope, changed your days,
Offering the job at Parkinson's and office ways,
So, babyhood, school, work - then becoming a wife
All milestones in your life -
Yes - off to church, a pony and trap ride -
Married in white, a lovely bride,
Marriage brought more joys and pleasure,
Three lovely daughters - each - a treasure,
Now! Another 'threshold', your 40th is here -
So step into another phase. And - enjoy it my dear.

Barbara Buckley

FOREVER OUR FRIEND

A new person entered our life, one sunny June day.
We knew instinctively, he was here to stay.

He enjoys his food, he's one of life's gourmets.
He's happy and healthy, who cares what he weighs?

He's got muscles and strength, but never been to a gym.
So no one in life, will mess with him.

He talks in a language, we often don't understand.
Would it be a dialect, from some other land?

He looks quite familiar, but that isn't bad.
Perhaps he acts like his mum, but looks like his dad.

Why are we tied to this person, whose life's just begun?
He is our one and only, baby grandson.

Our lives won't be the same, now that he's on the scene.
He's our *Charlie Albert* at number 14.

E M Napper

My Husband, My Friend

When I feel sad you make me smile
When I feel lonely you stay for a while.
When my days are dark you bring me light
When I am hurting you make it all right.

If I lost my sight you would be my eyes
If I were low you would be my highs
If I were hungry you would give up your bread
If I felt weary you would find me a bed.

All these things I would do for you too
Because our friendship is loyal and true
As my husband as well as my friend
I know that our love will never end.

Karen Barry

Ode To Rob And Samantha

(4/8/2001)

I think of you, morning 'til night all day
I think of you, whatever, come what may
I think of you, whatever you may do
I think of you, all day, just you

I think of you, when you're sleeping at night
I think of you, when looking in your eyes so bright
I think of you through good times and bad
I think of you when I'm happy or sad

I think of you when we disagree, you're still right
I think of you when we argue or fight
I think of you 'til my body goes numb
I will always think of you in time to come.

Sheridan Anderson

THE TELEPHONE CALL

He promised me he'd phone tonight.
He hasn't yet, still he might.
It's only half past eight.
That really isn't very late.
It's nine o'clock, oh God if you make him phone.
I promise that I'll never moan.
Again. I'll be so good.
I'll diet, honest, give up food.
And drink, none shall pass my lips.
I'll exercise, swing those hips.
If you've heard me God, let him phone by ten.
Then all will be alright again.
It's ten past ten and still hasn't called
Did you not hear me God at all?
I know he's never going to phone.
He's out with another while I sit here along.
Still I won't despair, there's more to life.
Oh God he couldn't be with his wife.
No, he told me that was over years ago.
And if he'd lied I'd be sure to know.
Wouldn't I?
Eleven o'clock, perhaps my phone is off the hook.
I think I'll just go and have a look.
No, all is well the operator says.
Perhaps I should just go to bed.
Forget the man, he's such a heel.
And really not worth this pain I feel.
Eleven twenty, the phone's still dumb.
I wish my heart could feel this numb.
I know he'll phone before I've read
This magazine, if not I'll really go to bed.
Forget the blighter, let him rot.
Unfortunately he won't care one jot.
That magazine was very small.
It didn't take much time at all.

Perhaps I'll give him one more chance more.
I'll have one more drink before.
I shut the door on our relationship.
It's midnight now and still no call.
He obviously hasn't thought of me at all.
I'll go to bed, lock the door.
Oh maybe I'll give him just ten minutes more.
The phone is ringing, such joy to bring.
He's four hours late. I'll let it ring.

Pamela Matthews

LOVE IS UNEXPECTED

When I set eyes on you, I didn't like you for start,
But you held hold of my heart and ripped it apart.
I couldn't believe it, I fell for it again,
Not realising it would cause such pain.
Love is unexpected and so controlling,
Visions of my heart choking and drowning.
Falling so low, beneath the ground,
A heart just waiting for happiness to be found.
It's not only affecting my heart, it's also my mind,
My soul, my eyes, visions without you are blind.
Dangerous as love can be,
Love is perfect no matter how much it's killing me.

Natalie Ellis

Soulmate

He is the one I long to kiss
He is the one I constantly miss
He is the fragrance I can always smell
He is the one to make my eyes well
He is the one that makes the world spin
He is the one that makes me sin
He is the one I could admire all day
He is the one I'd ask to stay
He is the one with deep brown eyes
He is the one to answer my cries
He is the one with which I walk on the sand
He is the one who holds my hand
He is the one I love to hold
He is the one to make me bold
What's brought us together is called fate
And he is eternally my soulmate.

Sophie Long

PURE LOVE

To gaze upon your radiant beauty,
And see the splendour of your eternal grace.
Brings forth my smouldering passion - not duty,
And those deep hid emotions, with ner a trace.

Your body's so perfect and so divine,
With radiance in abundance - bright and clear.
Like a deep and sensuous - perfect wine,
To outshine all earthly feelings, in tear.

You move so sensuous, so distracting,
With poise and posture - so demure.
Arousing my long smothered emotional reactions,
Promising my aching heart - a love so pure.

Gary J Finlay

THANK YOU

As the years just pass away,
My love for you just grows each day;
Your smiling, kindly, gentle face,
Shines forth each time I say my grace.

Those early years when children small,
You guarded, guided, them from falls;
Those camping trips beside The Lakes,
Made family life like ice on cake.

Through teenage years when problems rise,
You never shirked, you were so wise;
The children proud of loving mum,
You put them first, you beat their drum.

With further study, more time away,
The house was quiet, no one to stay;
The holidays brought lovely treats,
Together for meals, great food to eat.

The time then came for careers to follow,
The rooms at home became so hollow;
It took some years to come to terms,
For countless years without a perm.

Those hours of joy in castle walls,
Those lengthy walks near waterfalls;
A whole new life to share with each other,
Yet always thoughts of family and mother.

Although the 50 mark long past,
I know our love will always last;
Those thoughts and dreams which mean so much,
Are always present when you're in touch.

John Paulley

My Darling Bride

Come with me my loved one
To lands so far away
I'll get to know you loved one
And bear you on our way.

Today we'll go to Cornwall
St Ives to be precise
You are so fair my idol
My one true paradise.

You are my rose of sharon
My lily, oh so sweet
Your hair so sweetly auburn
Our lives together meet.

Today we stood before God's altar
We must never, never falter.

Janet Cavill

First Love

My first real love
Lived but a mile away
From school to home
Got later every day
I did cover some ground
But it was not to last
In fact the day came
Gone and oh so fast.

M D Bedford

ELIZABETH NORTH

The day I first saw you
My heart missed a beat
A more beautiful lady
I couldn't wish to meet

Your eyes have more sparkle
Then the stars at night
Beside your beauty
The sun doesn't look so bright

Your vibrant, intelligent
Beautiful and serene
I pinch myself, to make sure
I'm not in a dream

I think of you everyday
I admire you, in every way
You're the one I desire
Of you Elizabeth I will never tire.

P F Maidment

ANSWERS

Why did it happen,
How did it end this way?
For what reason was it,
And why won't you say?
Why do I feel so guilty,
When it was you who walked away?
Why is it me who's hurting,
For what reason won't you stay?
Please answer all my questions,
And put my mind at rest,
For I know that I deserve it,
For my love for you was blessed.
So why did it happen,
Why did it end this way?
For what reason was it,
And why won't you say?
For you know all the answers,
And you can set me free,
Free from all this heartache,
And you'll be free from me.

Steffen A P Lloyd

My True Love

My true love, I love you,
More than words can say,
I'll love you more tomorrow,
Than I do today.

I love you more tonight,
Than I did yesterday afternoon,
And I wish you to be my bride,
Very, very soon.

Next year, my love, will be uncountable,
I dread to think what I'll do,
If I cannot be married,
So that I'm even closer to you.

So now you've heard my feelings,
And know you're the love of my life,
Will you light up my world even more,
And say, '*You'll be my wife?*'

Marvyn Attwell

We Are A Rose

They say that love
Is like a rose -
If you hold too tight
It hurts then dies!

We are a rose
Bursting into flower,
Gently growing stronger
Each and every hour.

Patricia Orton

I Need You Girl

Every day I'm without you
I feel so sad
But when you're near
I feel real glad
And as the day fades away
I need you girl

Every night I sit and pray
To be with you
For one more day
My heart is lonely without you
All I want is to hold you
I really need you girl.

Simon McAlear

LOVE'S MELODY (SONNET)

Do you play my tune when you think of me?
Soft fingers wander on piano keys,
A love song played with sensitivity,
And striking a chord that is meant to please.
One note to another, love's stepping stones -
The music's so sweet that I drink its wine,
Harmony of sensuous overtones,
Its pleasure on my lips is so divine.
The words on their own do not make the song,
Treble and bass with their heartbeat of sound.
In the arms of music's where you belong,
Candlelit shadows slow-dancing around.
If my thoughts become words that embody,
My feelings for you are love's melody.

Olliver Charles

Don't Get Changed

I love her laugh
I love he giggle
I love my arms around her miggle
I love her tall
I love her all
I love her feet
I love her hands
I love the way she understands
I love her being juvenile
I love her radiating smile
I love her flattering attention
I love those bits one shouldn't mention
I love to look her in the eye
To not make I
Bend my shoulder
I love her wordage getting bolder
I love her words
I love her rhyme
I love her making good the time
I love her shapely aspen stance
I love her honest open glance
I love her voice
and gosh - I love her choice.

Seãn Jackson

My Girl

She walks like whispers on the wind,
Her hair a flowing mass,
Tiny golden straw-like ends,
Of summer meadow grass.

Her eyes of softest satin,
So dreamy in the sun,
They make you melt into the dreams,
Where you can have such fun.

Her slender form just seems to glide,
Like swallows in the air,
She passes with such tender grace,
As if you were not there.

Her captivation grabs you,
Dragging you her way,
No matter how you want to leave,
Her beauty makes you stay.

To speak to her seems daunting,
It could be such a mess,
How could you tell perfection,
Words cannot express.

Perhaps stay in the distance,
Let her walk on by,
Then think about the chances missed,
That could make you cry.

S Mitchell

One Day

I'm going to try and get you to say
That you really, really love me
But if you don't then I won't cry
Walk away or even ask why.
I'll just keep on keeping on
Just like I always have done
Deep down I'll still love you
Maybe one day you'll say you love me too.

If you're lonely I want you to know
You can call me on the telephone
Say exactly what you want to say
Reverse the charges - hell, just let me pay!
And if your boyfriend starts to treat you bad
That would make me really, really mad
Tear me up, right up deep inside
The thought that he would make you cry.

Where you walk I'm sure to follow
Because without you my life's so hollow.
And if you catch me staring at you
I don't care - it's only natural.
Being near you just isn't quite enough
Because it means that I cannot touch
The beauty that shines in front of me
But one day, just one day, maybe . . .

Timothy Cole

FOR JEAN - VALENTINE'S DAY 2000

I love you more and more each day,
I've always prayed 'twould be this way.
I thank God He gave you to me
And hope that it will always be.

I love you dear from head to toe;
Not just your body - oh dear me no!
I love your mind and spirit too,
You always thrill me through and through.

I love your funny little ways
They brighten up the dullest days.
The way you muddle people's names
And let me beat you at card games.

As I look back through all our years
There's much more happiness than tears.
I hope this new millennium brings
Many more delicious things.

Retirement came in '99
It seems to suit us both fine.
I've learned to cook an apple pie,
One thing I don't have to fry.

You know I'm blessed in all my life,
I have the most fantastic wife.
You've given me everything you can,
No wonder I'm your greatest fan.

So thank you love for all your love,
We seem to fit like hand in glove.
I hope the future brings us joy
From your devoted little boy.

Tony Olivey

FATE?

Was it fate that made me glance down the street?
To see that young man, so pretty, so sweet.
Was it fate, that I saw her again, the next day?
As she sat, sipping tea, in our local café.

Was it fate, that she stumbled and knocked over my drink?
As she stood there, embarrassed, I gave her a wink.
Was it pleasure I felt whilst we chatted away?
As we walked from the café on that warm summer day.

Was it pleasure I saw, when I asked for a date?
Her smile seemed to glow as we leaned on her gate.
Was this love I was feeling as we shared our first kiss?
My heart started pounding at such heavenly bliss.

Was it love, that I felt after nearly a year,
Of seeing her daily and holding her near?
Was our future ordained from that very first date?
Do you believe in love? Do you believe in fate?

Dennis Young

Perfection Of A Moment

She steals the distance of a dream
Her feelings sing a sweet lament
Like sunlight bouncing off a stream
The glinting iridescent beam
That never knew the way we went
How kind that time itself had leant

To us that hour heaven sent
A lifetime in a memory spent
Because that day our world was meant
To bring us freedom eminent
And in that truth we underwent
Perfection of a moment

My love you lie within the ground
And still I hear the song you sung
So deep inside still chants the sound
I taste your love upon my tongue
Within myself and all around
The happiness from you I found

First time I ever saw the sun
First breath of air inside my lung
Across all corners my love flung
A something new had just begun
I won't forget you friend
Because you died too young.

Sparky

THE MOST INFLUENTIAL WOMAN IN MY LIFE

She is patient, she is kind -
She gives me time to unwind
She offers me help which I refuse,
The wrong decision I always choose.

I want to apologise to my friend
I want our relationship to mend,
I want to tell you how much I love you
And that I appreciate all the things you do.

I feel bad when we fight -
I leave the house in a plight
I go through the bad things I have done,
The burden on my mind weighs like a ton.

You have helped me when I'm in need
You supply food when I need to feed,
I want to tell her that I do love her
Obviously I should because she's my mother!

Jodie McKane

THE MOMENT

Do you remember when we were as one,
When magic was woven which made our eyes shine
With hope for the future, it stretched on and on?
Well the future's arrived and the magic has gone.

Do you remember us lying and breathing one breath?
Our passion was so big it made our hearts stretch
With the joy in each other, but tears were to come
When the future arrived and the passion had gone.

We should nurture our dreams for they don't yet exist
And live in the moment, for it's like a brief kiss
Of a lover, once here and is soon in the past,
Its touch like a butterfly, fleeting and fast.

Our future's secure, for it's just in our dreams
So look to the present, it's not what it seems.

Dorothy Horton

Carly

Carly, you're the baby we wanted so much,
To hold, to love, to cherish, to touch.
We will all miss you with all our heart,
We wish we could have you and never be apart.
We will be thinking about you now and forever,
You will never be forgotten, not now, not ever.
You will always be my darling baby niece,
I hope you're with the angels, and will rest in peace.
Please may God take you under his wing,
A comfort to us we know this will bring.

Lorraine Hunting

BRAM

Darling this and darling that, how cheap endearments call,
But will she be your darling when backs are to the wall?
Bikini babes and busty blondes give lustful thoughts to men
But will they still be loving when we lose our basic yen?

Just one test beats all the rest, does she love you as she loves life?
Through joy and woe, now this I know is the credo of my wife.
She answers to a nickname, I simply call her 'Bram'
But I rarely need to call her, cos she's close by where I am.

I still gaze at the beauties, a saint is what I'm not
But I say a prayer to Heaven in thanks for what I've got.
And when we come to leave this Earth and find St Peter's grace
I've asked the Lord so many times to book a double place.

Denis M Pentlow

MY HUSBAND

We've been together, as they say
For more than 40 years,
And you have been my right hand,
The rock on which we stand.
Together we have built a life -
A kind of dynasty -
With love and trust and friendship,
Open for all to see,
This house we've grown together in
Has been home for 30 years,
Its sturdy walls have listened to
Many times of joy and tears.
I well remember when we bought it,
A pittance now you'd say,
But it took all our savings
With a bit left - put away.
The moment we came into it
We knew that it was right -
Some places have that atmosphere
Of warmth and love and light.
Our children were all born here,
The sons who make us proud;
We've learned with them and grown with them,
And cowered at music loud!
They've found their niches bit by bit
With many a backward step,
But we are always there for them,
Their rooms - in case - we've kept.
So mostly now it's me and you
To live our lives anew,
Enjoy forgotten interests,
And friendships old and new.

We've shared the years together
Been (almost) rich and poor!
But the highlight of my day is still -
When you come through that door.

Ann Dodson

A Rare And Precious Moment

Such trying times we'd gone through,
But stood by each other to give our due,
Now we needed something magical,
To make our hearts more musical.

Then I came up with a thought,
And we agreed we ought,
So the vicar I did approach,
And his ideas poach.

He agreed it was good,
And said he would,
So on with plans I went,
And told you in my letter I sent.

Then when you were home again,
After so much pain,
The aisle we did walk down,
Ignoring those who did frown.

Special words we vowed to each other,
In front of your sister and brother,
They meant far more than the first time around,
Giving my heart much joy to abound.

Now we will stay together always,
For the remainder of our days,
This is what love and marriage is all about,
'I love you,' with all my heart I shout.

Susan Shaw

My True Love - Martyn

My one true love has gone away,
Feels like forever and a day,
Upon my cheek lays a permanent tear,
He is far away, yet in my heart so near,
A part of me has gone with him,
An empty chasm he has left within,
Nothing can ever take his place,
His warm, gentle smile, his loving embrace.
An empty pillow lays beside me in bed,
With just an impression where he rested his head,
No one to hug and hold me tight,
No kiss to seal a peaceful night,
No words can express the depth of my love,
As each day descends from Heaven above,
And so I wait, until he returns to me,
Then fulfilled and contented I shall be.

Corinda Daw

CLOSE AND INTIMATE

He smiled at me across the aisle,
And I responded instantly;
How pleasantly I was beguiled,
I sent him back a smile from me;
Right from the start we got on well,
I laughed with him, we seemed to gel;
We made small talk - a little chat,
At first it was nothing more than that;
But when he took me in his arms,
Not a single sound was heard;
For what we felt for each other,
We didn't need a word;
We just held on - we didn't speak,
For the look in his eyes had spoken;
The 'can't you see I love you' way,
Is the sweetest sort of token;
From me to him and him to me,
Just started off as chemistry.

June Lane

TOAST

Love is . . .
Not the first flush of romance of our younger years
Or the different moods that makes for tears
Not the passion of new love
Or the sweat and the heat
Not the tingle in one's fingers
When two hearts meet

Love is . . .
What we have now, the thought and the care
No matter what I do I know you are there
The niggles and anger when I mock and I chaff
You wrap in a cuddle and make it a laugh
That's not a grey hair when you tell me I'm thin
No that's not a wrinkle, there's no spot on my chin

The look on your face when I tell you I'm broke
Money you spend to go up in smoke
Pride in your eyes when you think I can't see
Comfort I feel when you're talking about me
Resignation from you when I'm crunching my toast
Warmth from your body when my feet need a roast

Gail Sturgess

I Miss You

I miss the intimacy of being
intimate, and seeing
trousers over a chair,
or hung up. Anywhere
and everywhere nothing is complete.
Although everything looks neat
and tidy, and just so,
I miss your hello.

I miss another toothbrush next to mine,
your washing on the line.
Conversation, and determination to cope
when all seems lost and there's no hope
for the future. Although I try
to forget you, I wonder why,
any time of day, with nothing much to do
I think of you.

I miss long walks together,
in all sorts of weather,
a last minute decision,
without planning or precision.
All loose with laughter,
and coming home after,
tired, but happy to be,
just you and me.

I miss the sea, stretched out
before me, and all about
a sense of space and sky.
And in the distance as far as the eye
can see, deep stillness,
and harmony with a caress,
soft, and sharp as the sea bird's cry.
I missed your goodbye.

Helen Filipow

Tell Him About It

(To Charles from Rene)

All the time putting up with me.
(Coming home to have her tea?
Certainly not, good gracious me,
Early next morning more likely to be.)

Irene Tester

To My Darling, Dave

I know when you read poems, you like the ones that rhyme,
I'm writing this one just for you because I've had some time
To think of what you mean to me and how I love you so,
It's full of things that I believe you really ought to know.

You make me smile, you make me laugh and you help me enjoy my life,
You made me really happy when I became your wife,
You're a caring, loving, thoughtful, kind husband and best friend,
I know that whether I'm up or down, on you I can depend.

I love being in your company wherever we may be,
I love each little smile and touch and when you cuddle me,
I'm learning more about you as every day goes by,
Which makes me sure I'll keep loving you until the day I die.

Alison Salmon

Tell Him About It

I do wish I had told him
Just how wonderful he was!
I do wish I had told him
Before my sudden loss!
But life was quite a struggle
And the uphill road seemed long,
And, somehow, in the din of life,
I forgot 'love's old sweet song',
But I'm sure that when the time comes,
And I stand at Heaven's gate,
He will be waiting for me
And I'll know it's not too late
To put my arms around him,
And whisper there and then
That he is 'Mr Wonderful',
The loveliest of men!

Joan Leahy

DEAR HUSBAND

If you asked what I love best about you
It would be hard to answer, because I love you so,
Your caring ways
That brighten my days,
The hugs, kisses, holding hands,
Making me feel very grand.
All the ways you help and care
And all the things you with me share.
I love your build, your height,
Your strength and your might;
Your ups and downs,
Your smiles, your frowns,
Your hair, your eyes of blue,
I just love all of you.
I cannot really say what's best I love about you
Because, to me, it's all best - and I love you so.

Joan McLoughlin

WHY I LOVE HIM

I love my man because all the little things he does
come together to make one love that is really special,
like being there when I am low, he cheers me up and I feel good again.
Little ways he makes me feel special and when we are alone
spend time together, just being him, strong yet tender, caring, loving,
kind and also caring about me like no one else can.
The simple things like a cup of tea first thing in the morning,
a packet of cigs, little gifts, because he cares and shows it,
But most of all he is a man the best,
I love him and I know for sure he loves me.

Gillian Robson

Loving You

My dearest, darling, sweetest love,
I love you with all my heart,
When we're together, I feel the earth move,
I'm hit by 'Cupid's dart'.

I've felt affection for several men,
But I've fallen in love with you,
When we're apart - for you I yearn,
And my love will always be true.

You're my knight in shining armour,
And I long just to be your wife,
Everything about you I adore,
And I'll love you for the rest of my life.

Ours is a mature love, my darling,
It seems to mean much more,
Feelings and emotions - so moving,
And well worth waiting for.

D M Carne

The Twins

I have a grandson called 'Philip Foghorn',
His voice's been like that since he was born.
His brother Lewis is the quieter one,
But similarities exist in each twin son.

They mostly play together very well,
But when they don't, they're like bats from Hell.
They kick, they thump and violence flares;
Each does whatever the other dares.

Fortunately it doesn't last for long,
As they are happier doing right than wrong.
And soon their arms are round one another,
For they're twins, they're friends, brother and brother.

Ina J Harrington

MOTHER'S LOVE

Mother's love,
in the early days,
so full of compassion in so many ways.
Loving all your growing aches and pains away
till one day you're fully grown,
and you slip away,
to a life of your own.
And a mother's love,
is no longer your own.

Iris Davey

MOTHER

As a teenager in desperation
I blamed myself for your separation
Now I know that was not true
There was nothing either of us could do

The only time that Dad would come
Was when he was on the 'school run'
Or if I had misbehaved
It was his attention that I craved

Pretend to go to school but 'twag'
Hiding my clothes in my bag
But this had to stop as Mum got wise
Putting a stop to all the lies

I'd sneak outside when grounded
Through the window, leaving it guarded
Mum got custody, it wasn't that bad
But I wanted to live with my dad

With hindsight I can now see
That the court did their best for me
I am glad they chose that way
As I wouldn't be who I am today

So thank you Mum, I realise now
That I must have been a right 'little cow'
Now I have children of my own
I only hope that I have grown
Loving, caring, like another
And that is you - my mother

This poem is for you, so let's be fair
If love was money you'd be a millionaire

Jane Paddey

MY HUSBAND - JOCK

Sometimes I long to say just how much you mean to me,
It's not as though I'm really shy,
The words somehow won't come,
Your thoughtful ways, your loving smile,
They make every day worthwhile.

Maybe you think that I don't care,
Because I don't always say,
But every time I look at you,
I love you more each day.

For all my family you've been there,
You have shown them just how much you care,
Dependable, trustworthy, strong and true,
These are the words describing you.

A husband and dad to be there for us all,
To share with us each day,
For your happiness always we will pray,
A dear Scotsman through and through,
We all think the world of you.

C Wright

Song Of Love

If I had to write a song of love
to all the people I hold most dear
I know not on what score I'd say
I've loved you dearly for many a day.
My heart cries out for your loving touch
for the glance that says you know so much
for all the years when we shared the fun
when our hearts were happy, content with its sun
how does one say I love you dearly -
after all the years and you see more clearly.

Beth Spinks

FAMILY TIES

If family ties are more than blood,
are they then a-working towards the common good?
With those we hold in great affection
with whom we've made a strong connection?

The people we love and whom we're thankful for
and for whom we will always keep an open door.
Are our family then, our relatives and our friends?
Do we tie the knot and there it ends?

But what if these ties stretch much, much wider
That there's no such thing as a rank outsider?
The persecuted, the homeless, the oppressed, the abused,
These are all words we've heard and we've used.

And beyond each of these words is a human being,
Thinking, feeling, knowing, seeing.
Are they not also our family?
Am I not tied to them, as they are tied to me?

When my family are poor and sick and needy,
Will it not hurt us all if I am greedy?
Far better then to do what is right,
Where there is suffering, to find the courage to unite.

God is love and we are His family,
Let us pray for compassion and humility.
Lord grant me a humbleness of heart and strength to care,
That I might see my family everywhere.

Karen Link

Sons

Sons are someone who
love you no matter what you do.
They fight your battles, feel your pain
then they make you smile again.

They're into the music
that's in the in time,
can sing all the words
and know all of the lines.

They're amusing and funny
but joking apart,
when it comes down to feeling
my boys are all heart.

Their sporting skills just
fill me with pride,
and to have them around
makes me happy inside.

They're the faces I miss
when I'm sat here alone,
and without them around
it just doesn't seem home.

If you're listening up there
when the judgement day comes,
take anything but
the love of my sons.

Kathy Moore

My Husband

Oh, how I have loved you!
I have loved you with such depth
I thought that I might drown.
I loved you with such height
I made of you the crown
And pinnacle of all my being.
My eyes I loved you with
And you were all my seeing.
Your face, my joy, my light,
The very purpose of my sight.
My heart did leap anew
Each time I thought of you;
And at your absence rage
As though locked in a cage.
Those were the early days,
And now down all the years
Of learning you and knowing,
My love is stronger and still growing.

Frances Marie Cecelia Harvey

My Dearest Husband

Darling as I write this line
My fingers tremble to know you're mine
I feel just like a young new bride
Starting life together, side by side
To me you are the nucleus of my life
I'm so happy you chose me for your wife
You are still the one who I adore
The man that thrills me more and more
My heart still flutters when we kiss
And when we're apart how you I miss
My tummy still does a little dance
When suddenly I see you just by chance
To me your name means so, so much
I love your smile, your voice, your touch
When we are close, as close can be
I think of all you mean to me
The way you love me makes me feel
So wonderfully happy, warm and real
I love you for all the good things you do
I love you, my husband, for just being you
And through all the years that lie ahead
I'll not regret the day we wed
For on that day we joined as one
In unity as the earth, moon and sun
For without you there is no place for me
On this spinning world in eternity
Feel now a kiss that is warm and true
Full of the love that I have for you
Your arms enfold me, I'll leave them never
I'll always love you, forever and ever . . .

Dorothy Raddon

The Endless Search

I walked the streets, I searched the tower, trying to find your door
So that I could stand outside there and be close to you once more
For I felt driven onward, now try to understand
By something deep inside me, almost like a command

Even in my dreams, I searched and searched, but never found that door
As I made my way around and up and down, until my feet were sore
Yet long after you had gone therefrom, they said 15 on the first floor
And I went back again one day, just to look upon the door

It looked like all the other doors, as at it I stared
When through the empty, eerie silence, your voice I'll swear I heard
Now who knows what the years may hold and maybe some day,
like me, you
Will walk the streets and climb the flats and search for someone too.

Joan Magennis

The Dream Of My Life

The dream of my life
Who cares for all my needs,
I hope I make a wonderful wife
And together we will succeed.

Each day starts off with you on my mind
Making my day a great head start,
You are great, caring and very kind
Which makes you a great man with a golden heart.

I wish all your dreams come true one day,
Being a millionaire and living that life,
But I can't wait too long to say
Thank you God, today I am still his wife.

You can be funny and happy when stress-free
But those awful days of sadness do appear,
Saturday nights I can't wait to see
You sitting and enjoying the curry and beer.

I do love you so much,
Enjoying all my days with you,
I hope you feel this as such
And look forward to many more years too.

Kulwinder Kaur Dulay

Our Baby

Once upon a time, we were two,
Now I'm getting fat and that's a clue.
As months go by I look a sight,
Then I get into quite a plight.

One morning I get some terrible pains,
And as I look down and there are some stains.
I must get the doctor as quick as I can,
Or I will have to go in the van.

My labour has started, the baby is coming,
The midwife phones Bernard and he comes running.
A baby arrives and it is a girl,
Which has some hair with a curl.

I thank the midwife and the doctor also,
And sit up in bed and watch them go.
The health visitor will visit each day for a week,
I'll look after her myself when I'm in the peak.

We'll have to register her and give her a name,
We don't want to have one which is too plain.
'I know, we'll call her Pertrena,' I said,
And Bernard agreed as it went to his head.

At the local chapel we had her christened,
We had in the end made our decision.
Pertrena Tania is her name,
We put her photo in a picture frame.

The years roll on and time goes by,
It makes you nearly want to cry.
Now she has a child of her own,
I can't believe how she has grown.

Eileen Denham

Thank You

Dear, sweet and kind mother
You are the reason I live
And breathe today
You have done so much for me
I would like to show you how much
I appreciate your endless love.
You bought me into this world
And so generously gave me a life
You held me in your arms
And I kept you awake at night
You taught me how to walk
Without holding your hands
You held me close when I was alone
You punished me when I was bad
You protected me when I was hurt
You comforted me when I was sad
You pulled me up when I was down
You held me up high when I was low
You listened when I needed advice
You gave me warmth when I was cold
You gave me strength when I was weak
You taught me how to love
And forgive and forget
You were always there so I wouldn't fall
You showed me how to appreciate
The greater things in life
The life you so generously gave me
You made me the person I am today
And for that my dear mother, I thank you.

Shiuuli Mozlu

Mum And Dad

We take our parents for granted,
And assume they'll always be there,
To protect, love and guide us,
Show their concern and care.

We shouldn't get too complacent,
But lavish them with hugs and kisses,
As long as they're in my life,
I know what real bliss is!

Christine Nolan

Nanny Mabel

Sometimes she sits by the fire and dreams,
When the wind rustles soft in the eaves,
Of the happy days and treasured scenes
When children's laughter never ceased.

Sometimes she hears footsteps on the stairs,
Smells the fragrance of warm bath soap.
But when she looks, there is no one there,
Just shadowy ghosts of much loved hopes.

Sometimes a weight comes upon her knee,
A soft arm round her neck,
A whisper says, 'Nanny, play with me',
And she dabs her eyes, the tears to check.

Yet her memories are all of happiness,
Of loving joy-filled yesterdays,
Of those she knew and loved the best,
Who now have gone their own brave way.

Gordon J Hellier

GRANNY

I remember you with a smile
I miss you being around
I always admired your patience
Such strength, in you, was found
You cared for all your children
Had their total respect and love
And I believe that you're still there
Watching them from above
I keep your memory alive
Telling my children of you
Showing them photos of time past
Because their memories of you are few
I never knew my other grandmother
But I imagine her just the same
I feel proud to be your granddaughter
And prouder still to bear your name.

Ruth Connolly

My Heart

You are my heart
You are my home
The one I can come to
When I feel all alone

You inspire me to do great things
You are the one who makes my heart sing
I am so proud to have you in my life
My heart
My soul
My mother.

Gemma Doughty

FAMILY TIES

I have a friend called Sandra, she lives just through the wall,
When I need help or comfort, it's on her I sure can call.
She is an inspiration, a tower of strength to me
And nothing's too much trouble, it's plain for all to see.
She makes my life worth living, just to know that she's so near,
I really ought to tell her that I hold her very dear.
And as I live alone now, my dear husband gone to rest,
Dear Sandra is my pillar, she's just one of the best.
She has a lovely family who include me as their friend,
It really is supportive when a helping hand they lend.
There isn't many people who have a friend like me,
A gift so rare to cherish, she fills my heart with glee.
She truly is an angel as she helps do all she can,
Not just for me, but others too - she aids her fellow man.
So, when I say my prayers each night, I make a special plea
To ask the Lord to bless her for taking care of me.
I ask Him to look after her through good times and the bad,
To hope that in her daily life she's reason to be glad.
And as I sit and think of her and all she's done for me,
I know I'm not alone in life, I'm as happy as can be!

Margaret Garvie

To Mothers

No task too difficult, no word of complaint
Those trials and tribulations, the patience of a saint
Of a beauty that shone out without cosmetics or paint
This clean, healthy aroma of love permeates
A cuddle, a kiss when freely needed
Patting away pain and those sulks were depleted
Her radiance glowed as she lovingly tended and cared
We enjoyed every moment, especially at prayers

Attentive and concerned when grey situations dominated
Being a back bond she fended and retaliated
Teaching us how to behave in such crisis
She was so gentle and of course we were delighted
Supporting our infancy and those toddler years
Bathing away disturbances and allaying all fears
Such was our mother whose endless charm
Prevented so much, without her there would have been harm

Pondering today as we now have grown into adulthood
Recalling those treasured moments and memories not quite understood
Gone from this world, we remember her dearly
For all that love and care she gave us so truly, sincerely
Her imprint is with us as we inherit that dream
As with our own dear infants with a passion we glean
Thinking of Mother and her blessed tenderness
She was admired, one of God's chosen, considered one of the best

R D Hiscoke

Happiness Is

(Dedicated to Jim)

H is for happiness, that first smile of the day
A is for always there, and knowing what to say
P is for pleasure, and sharing it with you
P is for predictable and knowing what to do
I is for idiosyncrasies, yours make me want to smile
N is for nervous, when I walked up the aisle
E is for enigmatic, which is a feature that I adore
S is for surprises, you always give me more
S is for special, which you are without a doubt

Altogether they spell happiness and it makes me want to shout
That I'm so glad I met you and you asked me to be your wife
Thank you for making me happy and for brightening up my life!

Joanne Gilbertson

HAPPINESS IS . . . MY GRAN!

Knitting, swimming, tidying up
My gran is always busy,
Although her name is really Jean
We call her Busy Lizzie!
Watching her rush round and round
Makes me feel quite dizzy.
Rushing round the shops all day long,
Bringing me out with her,
She buys me lots of lovely things,
She is very fun to be with.

Corinne Pedley (10)

GRANDCHILDREN

Sunlight shimmers in sky above
Pearls of laughter, children at play
Offers a special gift of love
Remaining within forever and a day.

Hiding, crouched behind the door
Whispering instructive plan
Creeping over toy-strewn floor
This game they will not share with Gran.

Smiling faces surround the table
Eyes shine with pure delight
Paper trumpets joyously sound
Cares of the day take instant flight.

Christmas eve, bed early tonight
Stockings all hang in a row
No protests, not a single fight
Racing each other to bed they go.

Pictures imprinted on memory
Fading never through the years
Angelic faces around candlelit tree
Overwhelming joy-releasing tears.

Warm, tiny fingers touching my face
Soft kisses brush my cheek
Eternally no other place
Greater pleasures than these, could I seek.

Thelma (Slee) Thomas

Happiness Is My Grandchildren

Lisa, my oldest, she's shy and very loving
Katie, my tomboy, full of fun and caring
Jamie, my sporty one, he's thoughtful and kind
Robert, my little chatterbox, always happy and smiling
Bradley, my karate kid, mischievous and so full of love
Daniel, my gardener, is full of sunshine and happiness
Matthew, my bright one, with such a beautiful smile

All so different, but I love them all the same
Their love, smiles and happiness are mine to share
Even when I'm old, they'll always be there
To keep me company when winter nights draw in
They'll be far better company than a bottle of gin
I couldn't live without them and that's the truth
They remind me so much of me in my youth
But when my life has come to an end, as we all know it will
The love in my heart will be with them still
So I'll dedicate this poem to my loveable seven
Then I'll watch over them all from a cloud up in Heaven.

Patricia A M Lawson

Words Of Warmth

Perhaps you have never been told
that your heartbeat is a special treasure
which cannot be bought or sold,
not with diamonds that are forever,
nor with a mountain of gold.
I'm not trying to be good or clever,
I just want you to see what I behold,
for you and my thoughts are together,
and I would even be so bold
to say that no matter what the weather,
be it summer's warmth or winter's cold,
autumn's leaves or even spring's heather,
in my dearest memory, you, I will always hold.

Dale Mullock

ADAM JAY

I can run my fingers
Along thin air
And still feel the memories
Of your car parked there
In my heart we'll never fade away
It feels like I saw you just yesterday
Can't count the blessings or the times
You have come running through
My life and mind
It's not the things you've done for me
That makes me love you so
It's all the things I can do for you
That you may never know.

Natalie Sloper

Days Of Yesteryear

The ponds we fished and paths we plod together,
The sunny days that went on forever,
The summer frocks we used to wear,
With slides and ribbons in our hair,
Shining through,
Forever true,
Those golden days of yesteryear.

S Gray

MEMORIES

'Shall we go for a walk after tea?'
my husband Alan would say to me.
So I fed three sons, put on my shoes,
while Alan was listening to the evening news.
Pulled on my coat, combed my hair,
'We'll drive to the beach, then walk from there.'
The next day dawns, with wind and rain,
'Let's go out for a walk again.'
'Where can we go on such a day?'
'We'll watch the fishermen in Weston Bay,
I think I'll join them,' he would say.
'Let's go now, while the tide is in,
wear something warm,' and he would grin.
I pulled on my coat, combed my hair,
we drove to the pier, and walked from there.
I left the seaside, when I lost you,
a beautiful lake is now my view.
I pull on my coat, comb my hair,
you would have loved to have strolled down there.
I'll go for a walk, I say to myself,
it's marvellous exercise, good for your health.
I shut my door, set off down the hill,
are you coming with me? I know you will.
I started alone, when I turn I find
you're there, my darling, one step behind.

Shirley Monckton-Rickett

Old Acquaintance

I walked along the busy street,
Bags of shopping, tired feet,
Then I saw him standing there,
I wasn't sure, I stopped to stare.
Turning, he gazed into my eyes,
Recognition, glad surprise,
We stood together, hands were met,
Forgotten now, the crowds, the wet.

His face was older, sad and lined,
But the nose was well defined,
And the eyes were bright and blue,
Still the person that I knew.
We stood and chatted of yesteryear,
Of times remembered, still so clear.
Why oh why had we lost touch
When once we two had loved so much.

I was sad to see my dear friend
Alone, unhappy, uncertain as to the end.
Though I myself was all alone,
Husband, children, all now gone.
Through ups and downs and happy years
There was happiness, there were tears.
Now I am both plump and grey,
Getting through life day by day.

Impulsively I asked him round for tea,
Though surprised, he accompanied me
Back to my small but cosy flat,
I introduced him to my cat
Who sat and purred upon his knee,
My visitor stroked him all through tea.

We talked and laughed, time flew by,
We discovered each other again, he and I.
Through the weeks our love has grown,
We are content with each other, no longer alone.

Margie Fox

Did We?

Did we ride our bikes
And climb tall trees?
Play rough and tumble
And scrape our knees?
Did we play two-balls against a wall
And chatter on our way to school?

Did we fly high on swings up to the bar
And see purple hillsides from afar?
Did we skip together in a rope
And laugh our heads off
At a childish joke?

'Here! Lift your chin and let me see.
Do you like butter?
Yes!
Now you do it to me.'

Did we tell the time by dandelion clocks?
Keep caterpillars in a cardboard box?
Did we search the grass for a four-leafed clover?
Make daisy chains 'til the summer was over?

Did we?

Carol Middleton

VALENTINE'S DAY 2000

If I should take my pen to write a line
of foolish verse - an old cliché,
a reminder of St Valentine, to say
I love you, in a vacuous self-conscious way.
Or even write a hundred lines
to cover all the Valentines we've known -
I would. But could that serve
to give you all that you deserve
in love and gratitude for all the years
you gave unstinting love - and facing fears
and trusting God?

You built a rampart tried and tested
about the things that we held dear
and made a home no matter where our fortunes rested -
and kept our children safe -
and gave them of your nature
sure foundation.
To live in trust and not lose sight of God.
And pass this grace to yet another generation
that, by being blessed will bless in turn
the children of our children's children.

And thus your patient and enduring love
will earn relief from future fears
to bring hope and peace through coming years.
And so this day of Valentine -
this is my prayer -
that God will bless you through the elder years
that you might rest in gracious merit won
and I might walk within your shadow
till twilight comes and all our days are done.

Derek Nevil Thorp

My Best Friend: For Amy

You are my best friend
My saviour, my ecstasy
I want you to know
You are the one that saved me

You have always been there for me
Whenever I needed you
You have always looked out for me
Whenever I'm feeling blue

We've both been through a lot
No doubt that's true
Our friendship is the one thing we've got
I couldn't live without you

We've always got each other
To act silly or mature
To drink cider with your mother
With you life is never a bore

We can play silly little games
Or take the dogs to the park
Some of the things we have done, oh the shame
Especially after dark!

Although we will never be perfect
One thing will always be true
To me you will always be worth it
Just remember there's always me and you

Kayleigh-jo Brittain

BEING WITH ONE'S WIFE

What a pleasure, is this life,
When one can spend it,
With one's wife!
Especially if she's young and sweet,
Just being with her,
Is such a treat!

A good wife makes life such a joy!
Just every moment,
You'll enjoy!
Seeing her smile at you, each day,
Keeps you happy,
One would say!

Being apart, it's just not fair!
When you love her,
And you care!
That's why happiness is life,
When you can spend it
With your wife!

Ron Bissett

Goodbye

Loving mother, caring companion, my dearest friend
Cherished mother, my heart won't mend
Those lonely nights anticipating that call
'Sorry dear, your mother's taken a fall'
Lights are flashing, sirens pierce my ears
Holding my mother's hand I try to hide my fears
The cubicle's like a prison with its ghostly drapes
Voices echo then a stainless trolley snakes
My mother cries, 'I want to go to sleep,'
I'm out of my mind and I uncontrollably weep
On the ward, all these old people are lying in straight lines
And over their beds hang these terrible signs
Nil by mouth, Doctor so-and-so, or just their name
And every single bed looks the same
They put drips into my mother's skinny little arm
I'm out of my mind and nurses try their best to calm
But unfamiliar objects are everywhere, it's all so strange
Orderlies are fussing around as Mum's covers they rearrange
On Thursday, all the family members assemble
My daughter reads the twenty-third psalm, her hands tremble
Her grandson is so bewildered, he tearfully leaves
White shrouded curtains hide a family that grieves
I touch my mother's sweet face and I say goodbye
Now I must face life without her, I break down and cry
The house is overwhelmed, with family members, neighbours and dear friends,
With beautiful wreaths and such wonderful messages they send
Goodbye dear, sweet, wonderful Mother.

Ann Hathaway

My Little Girl

Paper and paste and paints and toys
And scissors and string and lots of noise,
Urgent and vital, she can't stop now
'Cause she's making a toy, with furrowed brow.
Her big brown eyes beneath her fringe
Hurry her hands as she grips the things
That will make her ideas come to life -
If the paste won't stick there'll be such strife.
Then all of a sudden - creation done
She shows her brother, my little son,
The thing she's made. Then, with cries of 'don't touch'
Scurries back to her room, it tight in her clutch.
When safely away in the untidy mess
Of books and puzzles, a shoe and a dress,
She runs down again and out to play
To her own little garden, now mostly clay,
Where little men made a day ago
Of mud and matchsticks, an acorn or so,
Lie back in the mud, back in the land
From which they were fashioned by her little hand.

Transient now her creations may be,
But will one day she who is part of me
Create and reflect in her own special way
Some depth of what this life has to say?

Douglas Bryan Kennett

TO A FRIEND

This is to a friend who is faithful,
This is to a friend who never leaves your side,
This is to a friend who kept my spirits up when they were low,
This is to a friend who never lets me down,
This is to a friend who loves me like no other,
This is to a friend who tries her best no matter the task
This is to a friend whose spirits are never low,
This is to a friend who wouldn't harm,
This is to a friend who keeps me warm in the bitter cold,
This is my K9 friend, Billie.

Emma Phillips (16)

My Mum

My mum is sweet and caring, just as every mum would be,
But I have just realised there's something I ought to see.
She's more than just my mum, she's a part of me.
She has an important role throughout my life,
Only for the sake of me.
We're both very alike and share our emotions together,
We share our secrets with one another, just like best friends do.
She's thoughtful and passionate and filled with sweetness.
I think we ought to realise that there's nothing more sweeter
than our mums.

Aria Habibi (14)

What's This

What's this, a friendship, you say!
Well actually, I'd call it a very special friendship.
You're always there for me in times of need,
even when I'm angry, not once have you let me down.
We have so much fun together, skating and shopping,
yeah that's us, two special friends.
I've never really had a friend like you before,
someone I can trust, knowing you won't say a word,
I take that and respect it, cherish it with my heart, and
I hope one day you'll do the same.
Look back at all the good times and on all those memorable times
and remember mates are around forever,
right now I think I'd better go, but before I do,
I want to mention, you're my very special friend
and I'll never let you go . . .

Rachael Elizabeth Howard (16)

MY MUM AND DAD

My mum and dad are very special to me.
They helped me and my brother survive the open world.
Librans at heart.
Born on the same day.
However, three years apart.
Mum, a Virgoan.
Ha!
More a Scorpio,
But no birthday under the
Passionate
And enthralling force of Scorpio,
Nevertheless, a Virgoan she is.
No shyness.
Nor diligence.
But stinging strictness.
Funny.
A detailed, minutiae tongue.
Dad, an Aries.
Good day.
Confidence.
Quickness.
Overload of risky fun.
Dynamite fun.
Fast rides.
No reaction to the neck-breaking speed.
Just calm.
Just laughing.
Just waving.

Christopher Gaunt (14)

Are You There?

Are you there when I send you my calls,
When I ask you for help and advice?
Are you there as my father and friend,
Or as my mother, so gentle and nice?
Are you there when I want to talk,
About this life so hard?
Are you there to help my problems,
And stop me being scared?
Are you in the holy heavens,
Or the great dark depths of Hell?
In the beauty of the Summerlands,
Or are you just a story to tell?
Whoever, wherever, if ever you were,
I'd hope you'll answer my call.
For you're the one and only,
My Lord, my lady, my all!

Richard Thompson

MOTHER

A silent whisper
A gentle sigh
That's how fast
The time's flown by

Here we stand
After all these years
After laughter and joy
After heartache and tears

Precious moments
We've shared from the start
Locked in my head
Locked in my heart

A special kind of bond we share
A special friendship
So strong and rare

A shining spirit
Not easy to find
A mother's love
So pure and kind

I thank the Lord
In His kindness and grace
For the day I was born
And looked up at your face

Nancy Pavlides

Grandma

(Written in loving memory of Amy Knightly, my grandma)

She had a long and busy life
She was a travelling show-woman
And a mother, grandmother
And wife

I never really knew her
She used to stay over at weekends
Her own room
When I was young

Then she stopped staying over
She visited on Sunday afternoons
She sat and talked
I avoided her

Then she couldn't come anymore
We visited her in the home
Lying in her bed
I shouted for her to hear me

We saw her one last time
She couldn't get better
She was very ill
I cried, the lump in my throat

I wasn't allowed to go
To her final goodbye
I should have wanted
To be with her more

Grandma, why did you have to die?

Laura Knightly (13)

As Time

As time slips slowly by
More and more it seems to fly
As the tides are slowly turning
There is more and more that I am learning.

As time slips further away
The more I wish to stay
But there is one thing that I wish to say
You're my best friend and that's how you'll stay.

Rachael Shanks (13)

THE WORLD'S GREATEST MUMMY

She's never heard this from me,
What I hear and see,
She does nearly everything for Shane, Grant, Scott, Abbie and me,
She's the greatest mummy.

She washes my clothes and she doesn't have time to moan,
She's not like my dad who lets out a groan,
She's the greatest for loving me,
She's the world's most brilliant mummy.

T B Manning (10)

THE BEST BROTHER IN THE WORLD

My lovely brother
I do like to smother
With kisses
And bless him with wishes.

My lovely brother
Is cared for by our mother,
When it's time to play he runs around
And makes a lot of sound.

He doesn't like healthy food
But give him junk food
Like biscuits and chocolates,
He'll gobble them down without any 'ifs' or 'buts'.

My brother likes to have a good lay
When it's time to get up on a school day,
But on Saturday or Sunday
He's up and away. (Even on a holiday.)

He needs a good rest
To be a good pest,
So to be a beautiful sight,
He needs an early night.

Hartinajit Kaur Dulay (10)

My Loving Mum And Dad

This is about my dad
Who never gets mad.
He likes to get his jobs done
With his loving son.

This is about my mum
Who blazes in the sun.
She likes to keep fit
And then likes a long sit.

Now about my dad
Who never gets sad.
He always asks me
To make his special cup of tea.

Now about my mum
Who likes to have fun.
She bakes us a cake
And when we're silly she says, 'For God's sake.'

Karandip Kaur Dulay (9)

My Special Grandma

Who is the person who is always kind,
More than any other person you'll find,
Will never leave anyone without hope?
Without her how would dear ones cope?

Who is the person who will never deny
Any life that is in need?
Who never is full of greed?
Who will always care?
Even in desperate times,
My grandma will always share.

Who will never stop loving me?
Who cannot be replaced?
Miracles are born from her face,
To make her my special 'grandma'.

Indresh Umaichelvam (12)

My Loving Wife

As I rock back in her old rocking chair,
I stare at the stars and think of Claire,
My loving wife with long, silvery hair,
She died in my arms about this time tonight.
I'll never forget her for the rest of my life,
We were married for fifty years or more,
She is the only woman that I ever adored,
She was the mother of our four kids,
Two sons and two daughters who thrilled us to bits,
They made us laugh and they made us cry,
But we all cried when Mama died.
We are close, my kids and me,
They don't realise, they don't see,
That I am lonely without my Claire,
Her rocking chair is empty and bare.
I picture her sitting in her rocking chair,
Stitching and sewing and combing her hair,
Our grandchildren hearing her sing,
And I would whistle and join in.
I'm getting old and tired and weary,
I just want to be with my girlie,
Up there above where the stars are shining,
Please take me with her to that silver lining.
As I rock back in her old rocking chair,
I stare at the stars and think of Claire,
My loving wife with long, silvery hair,
Waiting to take me with her up there.
My heart is broken in a thousand pieces,
I cannot bear it, I cannot release it,
Twelve months have passed and it still creases.

I love my children very much
It breaks their hearts in two
To see me suffer, to see me cry,
They know I won't be happy until I die,
And once again be at my wife's side.

Gillian Corbett

My Mum

From when I wake up in the mornings,
To when I go to bed at night,
My mum is always there for me,
She has a gentle touch.

She makes my lunch for me to take to school,
She cooks and cleans and washes my clothes,
She listens to what I've got to say,
Her answers are nearly always right.

She takes me home from school each day,
She takes me to the youth club on a Friday,
I love my mum and my dad
They are the best in the whole *universe.*

Judith Culbert